EMOTIONS and FEELINGS

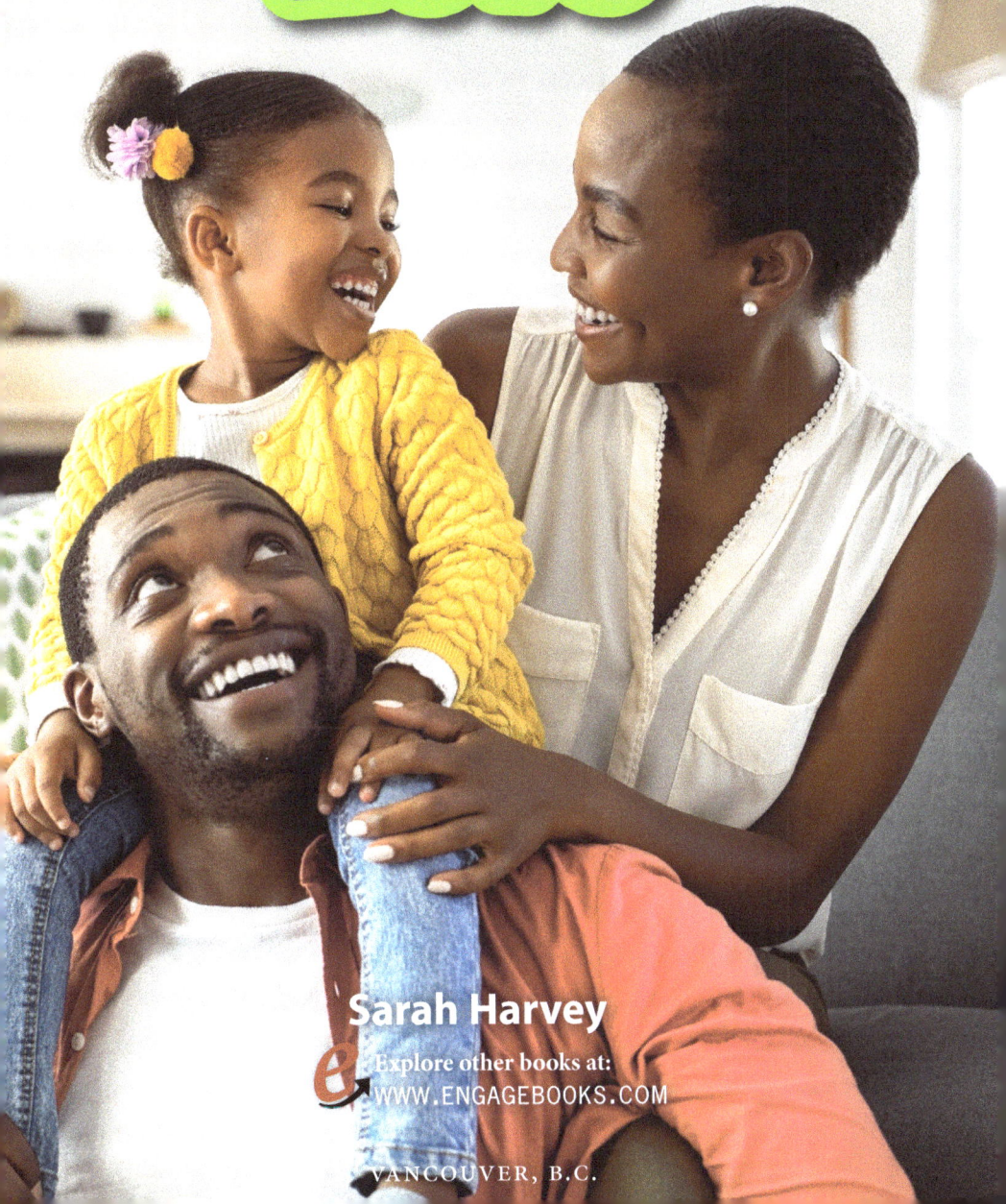

Love

Sarah Harvey

Explore other books at:
WWW.ENGAGEBOOKS.COM

VANCOUVER, B.C.

WWW.ENGAGEBOOKS.COM

Love: Level 1
Emotions and Feelings
Harvey, Sarah 1950 –
Text © 2023 Engage Books
Design © 2023 Engage Books

Edited by: A.R. Roumanis, Ashley Lee, Melody Sun,
and Sarah Harvey
Design by: Mandy Christiansen

Text set in Arial Regular.
Chapter headings set in PeachyKeenJF.

FIRST EDITION / FIRST PRINTING

LIBRARY AND ARCHIVES CANADA CATALOGUING IN PUBLICATION

Title: Love / Sarah Harvey.
Names: Harvey, Sarah N., 1950- author.

Description: Series statement: Emotions and feelings
Identifiers: Canadiana (print) 20230447333 | Canadiana (ebook) 20230447341
ISBN 978-1-77878-155-1 (hardcover)
ISBN 978-1-77878-156-8 (softcover)
ISBN 978-1-77878-157-5 (epub)
ISBN 978-1-77878-158-2 (pdf)
ISBN 978-1-77878-159-9 (audio)

Subjects:
LCSH: Love—Juvenile literature.
LCSH: Love in children—Juvenile literature.

Classification: LCC BF723.L69 H37 2023 | DDC J155.4/1241—DC23

This project has been made possible in part
by the Government of Canada.

Canada

Contents

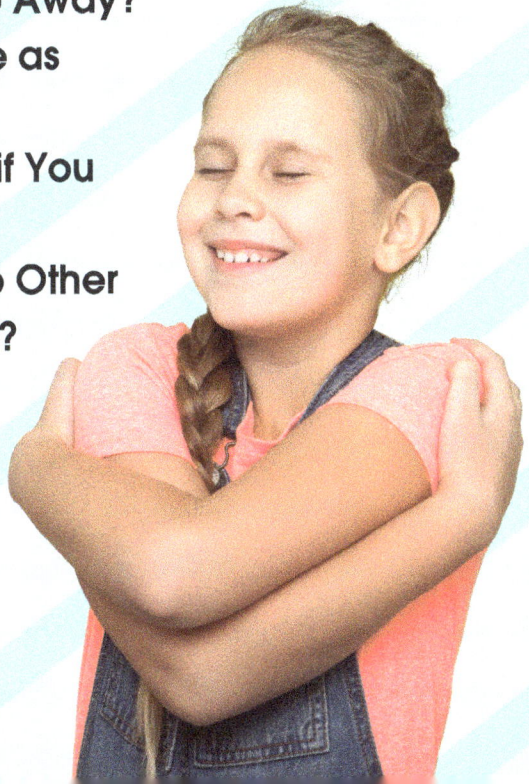

What Is Love?

Love is an emotion. You feel it when you really care about someone or something. Love keeps people **connected** to each other.

4

Love is not just a feeling. It is an action too. When you love someone, you want to do things for them and with them.

Loving yourself helps make you really good at loving others.

5

Why Do People Feel Love?

People often feel love when they **trust** someone. You love other people even if those people make mistakes or do things you do not like.

You might love your mom because she always helps you. Even if she gives you a time out, you will still love her. She will still love you too.

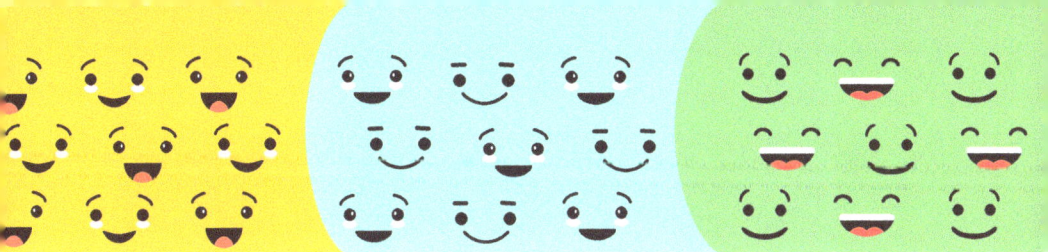

Are There Different Kinds of Love?

There are many kinds of love. You can love a person, a pet, a place, or a thing. Each kind of love will feel different.

Everyone has a different way of showing their love. One person might use words to tell someone they love them. Another might give hugs.

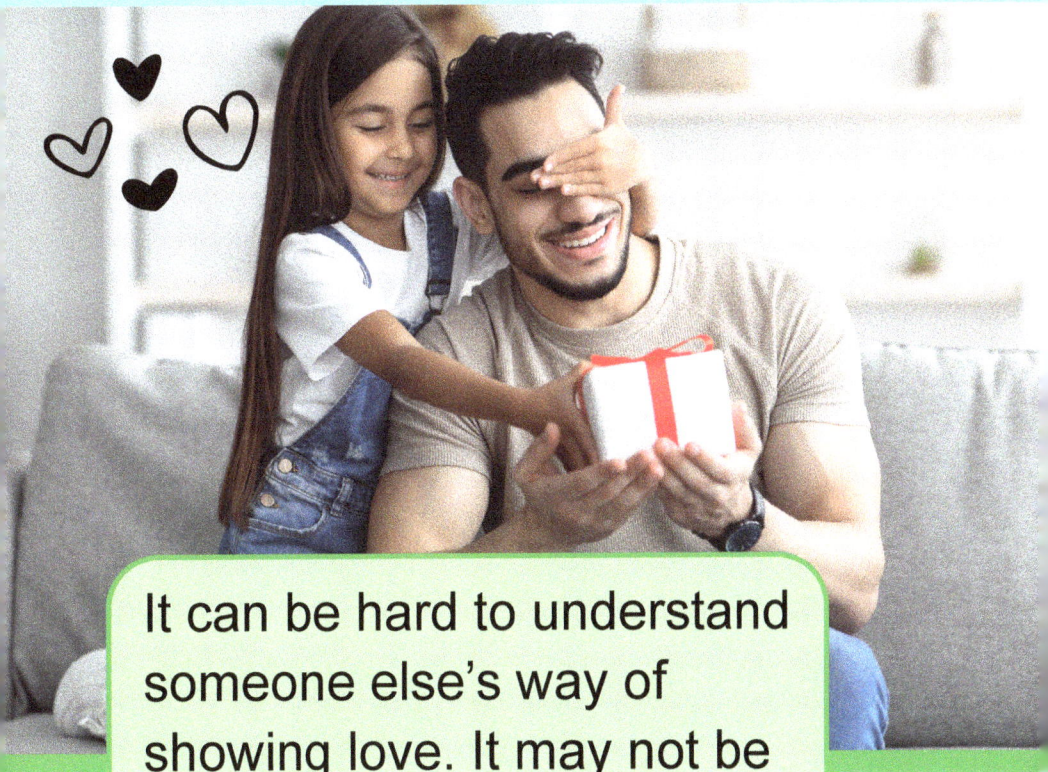

It can be hard to understand someone else's way of showing love. It may not be the same as yours.

9

How Does Love Affect the Way You Think?

When you love someone a lot, you think about them often. It may be hard to stop thinking about them.

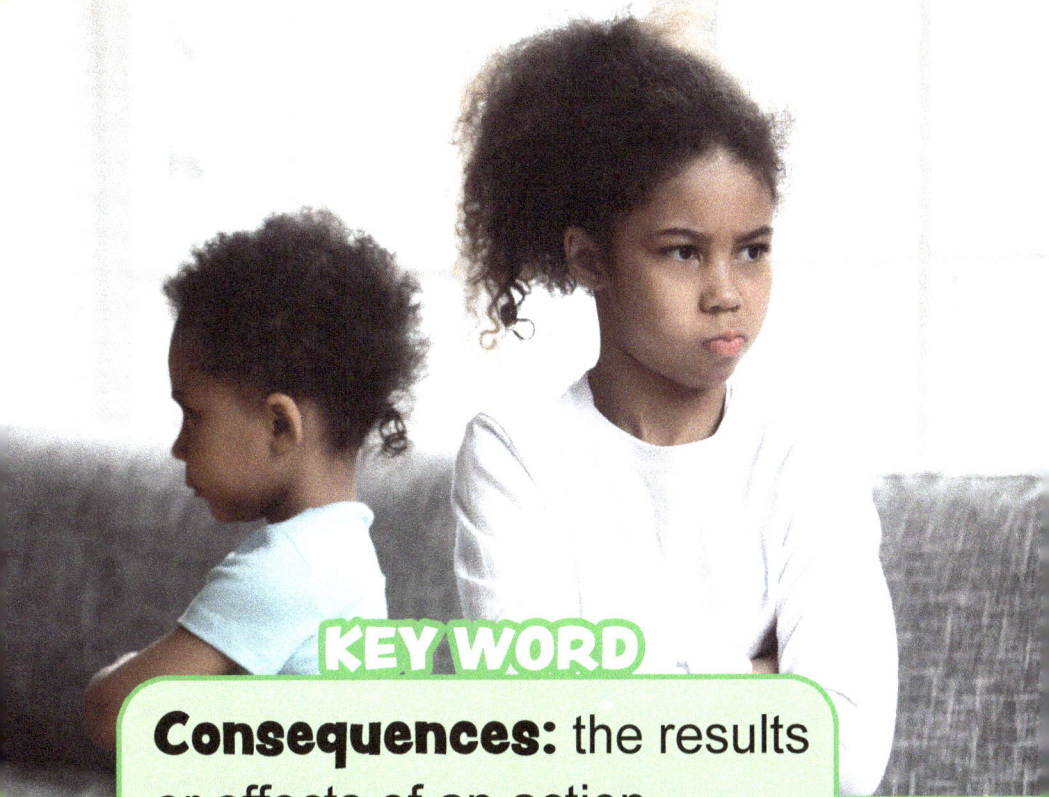

KEY WORD

Consequences: the results or effects of an action.

Some people may make bad decisions when they love someone. They only think about making the other person happy and forget about the **consequences**.

11

If you have a fight with a loved one, love can help you forgive them more easily.

How Does Love Affect the Way You Act?

Knowing you are loved makes you want to be kind and helpful. You want to share the love with others. You want them to be happy.

Love can make you want to do things you do not enjoy. You might have a friend who loves camping. Even if you do not like camping, you may go with them to show how much you love them.

Is Love Ever a Bad Thing?

Sometimes love can take over a person's life. This is called an **obsession**. It is not healthy for anybody.

Obsession: when something or someone is always on a person's mind and nothing else matters.

Some parents try to control every part of their child's life. They see it as a way of showing their love. It makes it hard for the child to learn to think or act for themselves.

Does Everyone Feel Love?

Most people feel love and give love. Love for a child can start even before the child is born. The love between parents and children can last a lifetime.

People who have had a hard life may not trust anyone. This makes it hard to give love and accept it from other people.

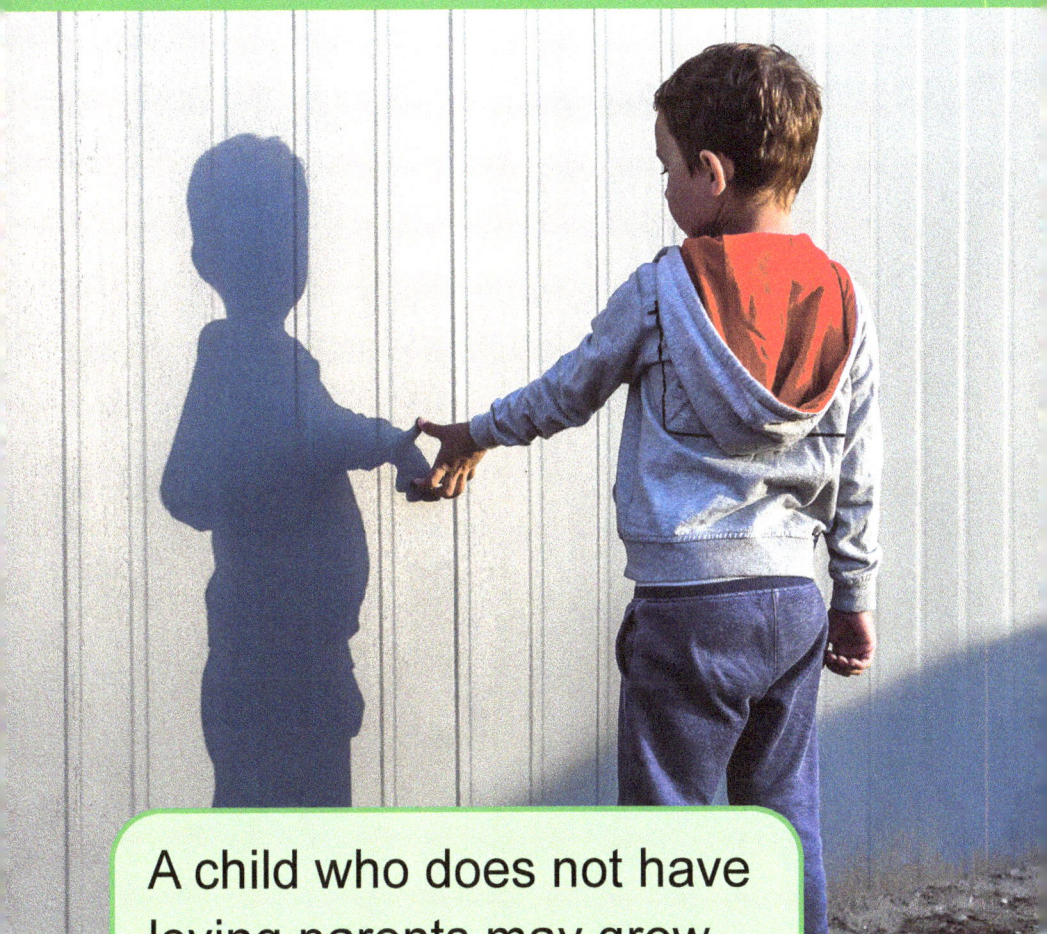

A child who does not have loving parents may grow up to feel angry and lonely.

What Does Love Feel Like?

Love feels different to different people. Most of the time, it makes people feel happy. It can also make them feel warm.

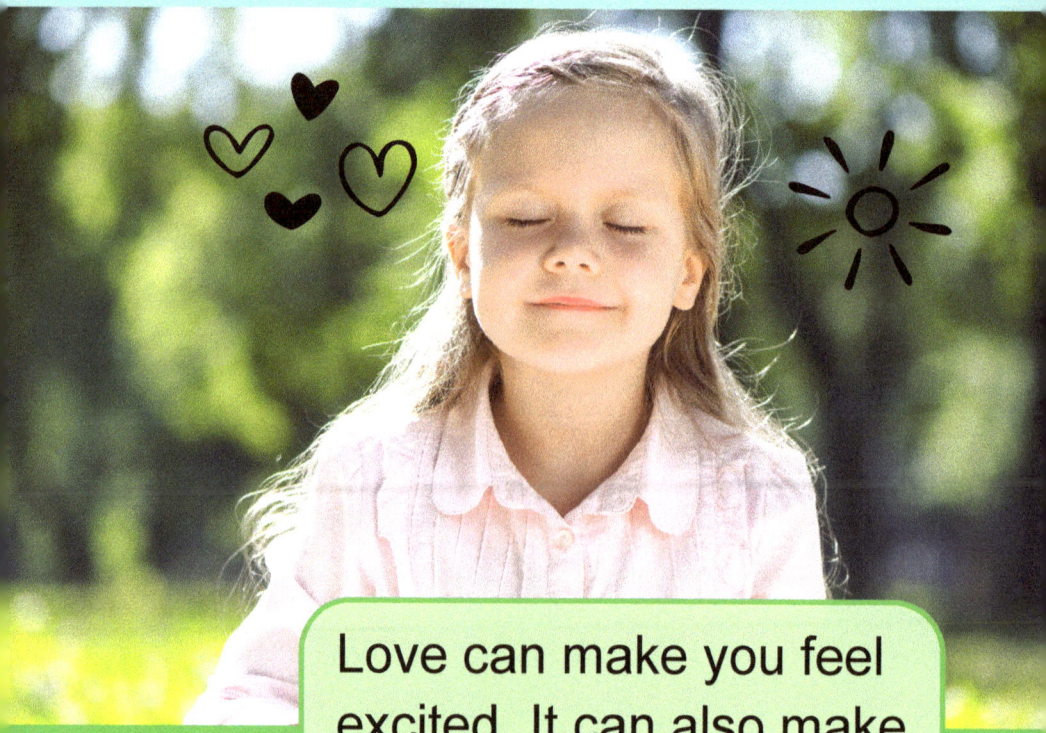

Love can make you feel excited. It can also make you feel calm.

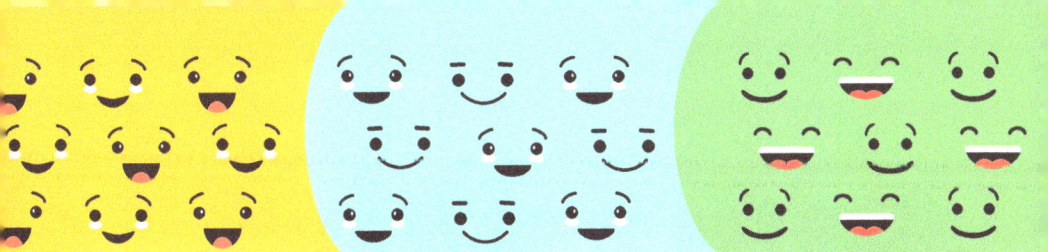

Love can lead to other emotions like hope and **gratitude**. It can make you feel safe.

KEY WORD

Gratitude: the feeling of being thankful.

Can You Make Yourself Feel Love?

You cannot force yourself to love someone. But you can make an effort to get to know someone better, and that may lead to love.

It can be hard to love others if you do not love yourself. Learning to love yourself can make it easier to love others.

It may be hard to love a step-parent at first. Spending time with them can make this easier.

Does Love Ever Go Away?

Love can last a long time. Some friendships last from childhood to old age. You may love your family your whole life.

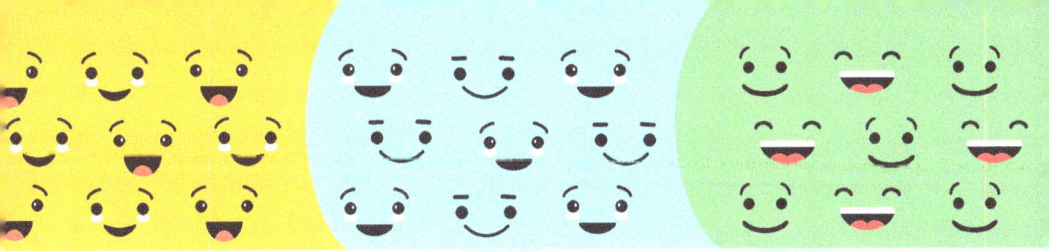

Sometimes love only lasts for a short time. You may stop loving someone or something. This is not always a bad thing. Sometimes people just grow apart.

You will be sad if someone you love dies or a friendship ends. This is called grief.

23

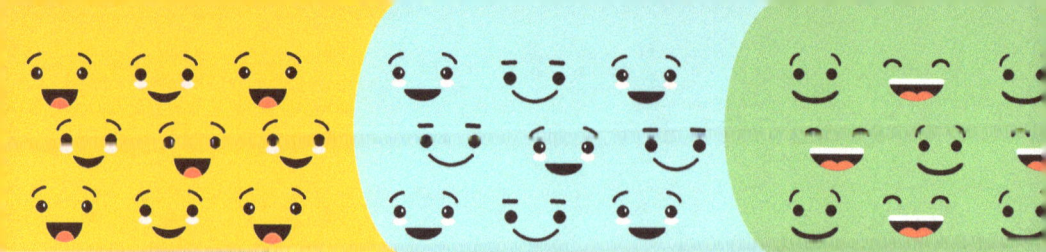

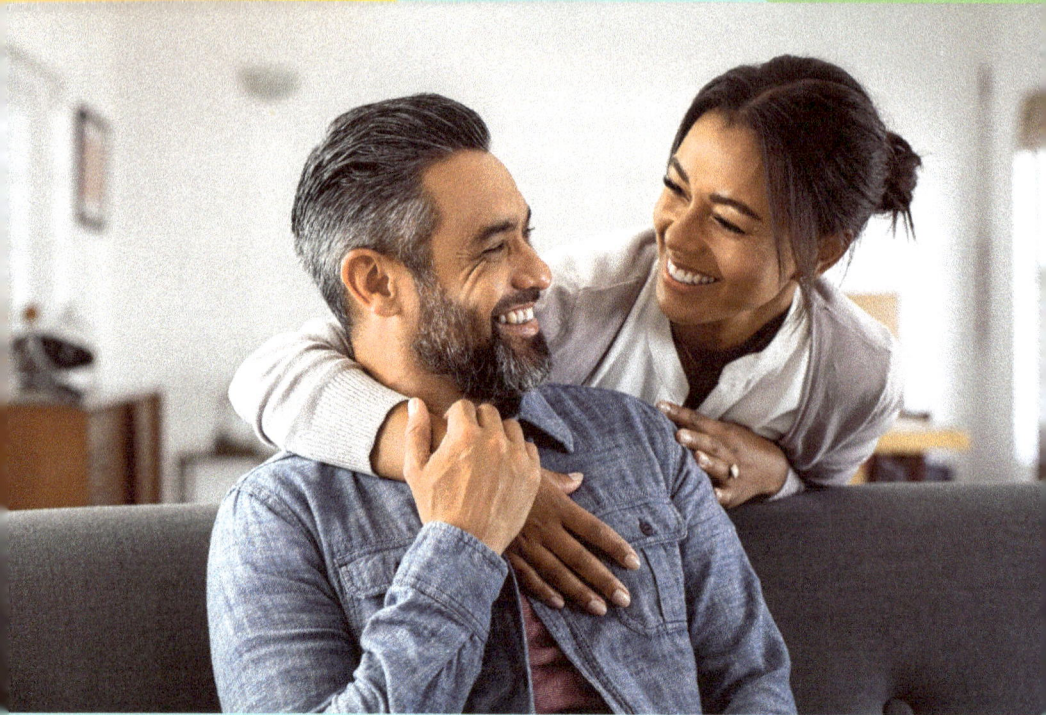

Does Love Change as You Grow Older?

Getting older often helps people understand love better. You may feel different kinds of love as you grow up.

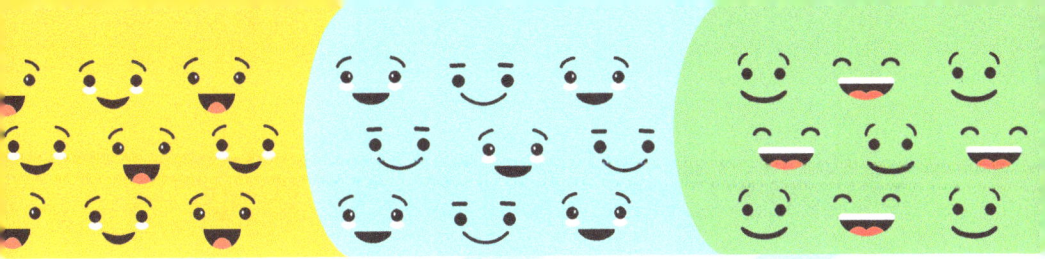

Most people learn to love new people and things as they age. You may find a new hobby or meet someone you want to marry.

When adults are in love, they want to spend their lives together.

What Can You Do if You Feel Unloved?

If you do not love yourself, take some time to get to know yourself better. Write down all the things you like about yourself. Try not to focus on the things you do not like.

KEY WORD

Unloved: not loved.

If you feel **unloved** by someone else, talk to them. Tell them why you feel this way and what would make you feel better.

Always ask if it is okay to give someone a hug. Some people may not want to be touched.

How Can You Help Other People Feel Loved?

It is good for people to know you love them. Tell your friends and family how you feel. You could get them a gift or give them a hug.

Be kind to the people you love. Do nice things for them even if they do not ask you to. Help your mom do the dishes or help your friend carry their books at school.

Quiz

Test your knowledge of love by answering the following questions. The questions are based on what you have read in this book. The answers are listed on the bottom of the next page.

1 What helps make you really good at loving others?

2 Are there different kinds of love?

3 What does knowing you are loved make you want to do?

4 What other emotions can love lead to?

5 Is it bad to stop loving someone or something?

6 What should you always do before giving someone a hug?

Explore other books in the Emotions and Feelings series.

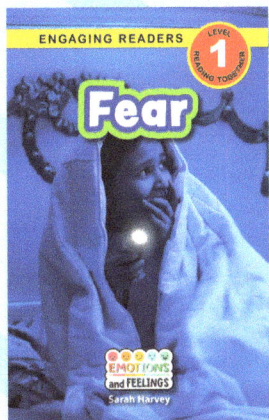

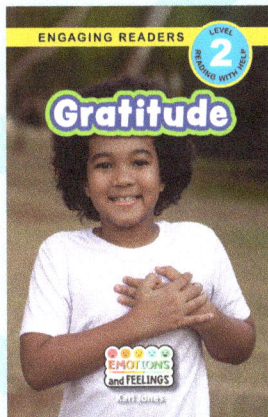

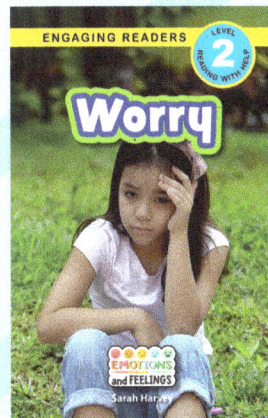

Visit www.engagebooks.com/readers

Answers:
1. Loving yourself 2. Yes 3. Be kind and helpful 4. Hope and gratitude 5. No 6. Ask if it is okay

www.ingramcontent.com/pod-product-compliance
Lightning Source LLC
Chambersburg PA
CBHW051238020426

42331CB00016B/3431